Going to See the Doctor for a Check-Up Visit
A Book to Help Manage Expectations for Children and Adults with Autism Spectrum Disorder

Kristine Kenny, MSN, RN, CPN, CAS
Illustrated by Madelyn Hess

Going to See the Doctor for a Check-Up Visit:
A Book to Help Manage Expectations for Children and
Adults with Autism Spectrum Disorder
COPYRIGHT © 2022 BY KRISTINE KENNY

ISBN-13: 979-8-9870047-0-8

Printed in the United States of America

Illustrated by Madelyn Hess

Going to See the Doctor for a Check-Up Visit
A Book to Help Manage Expectations for Children and Adults with Autism Spectrum Disorder

Use this space to tape a picture of your own doctor's office.

We encourage you to tape a picture of your own doctor's office on the cover of this book as well.

Kristine Kenny

This book is about going to the doctor for a well visit.
The doctor wants to make sure you are healthy.

When you get there, you will go to a waiting room. You will have to wait until it is your turn to see the doctor.

When it is your turn, you will leave the waiting room with your mom, dad, or caregiver with a nurse.

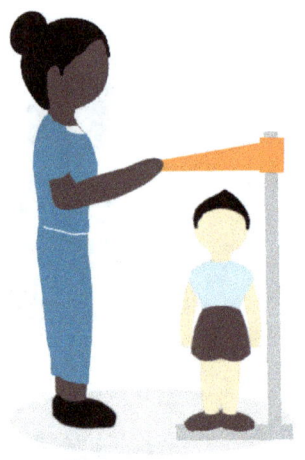 

The nurse will check your height and weight.

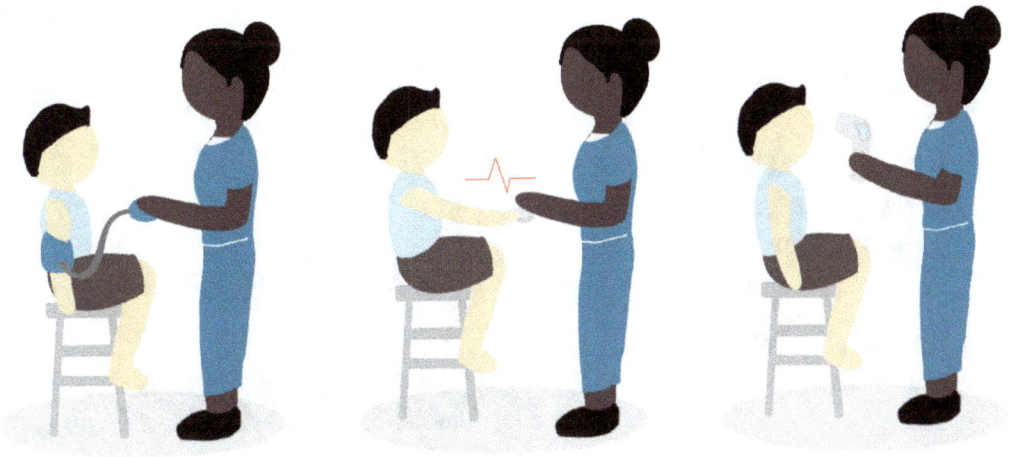

The nurse may check your blood pressure,
temperature, and heart rate.

Next, you will get to go to your own exam room.

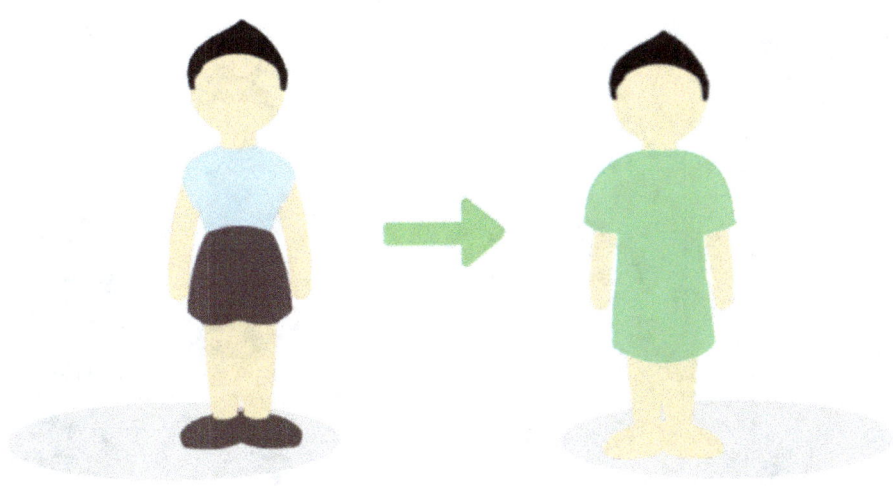

Here, you will get ready to see the doctor.

When the doctor comes in, they will talk with your
mom, dad, or caregiver and you about how you
have been doing.

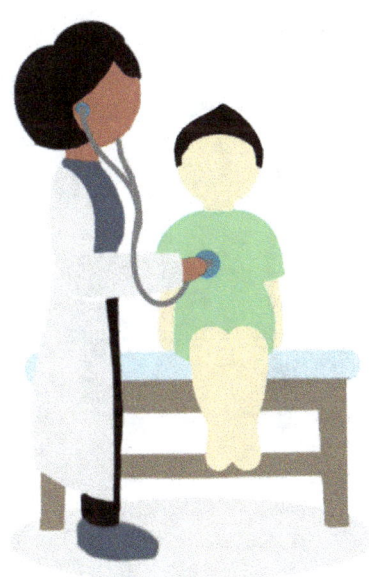
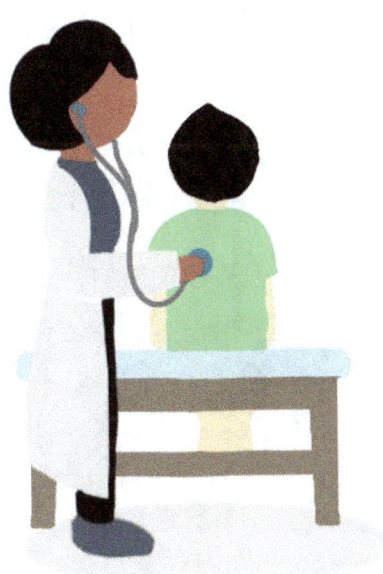

The doctor will listen to your heart. The doctor will listen to your lungs. You may need to take some deep breaths in and out to help the doctor listen.

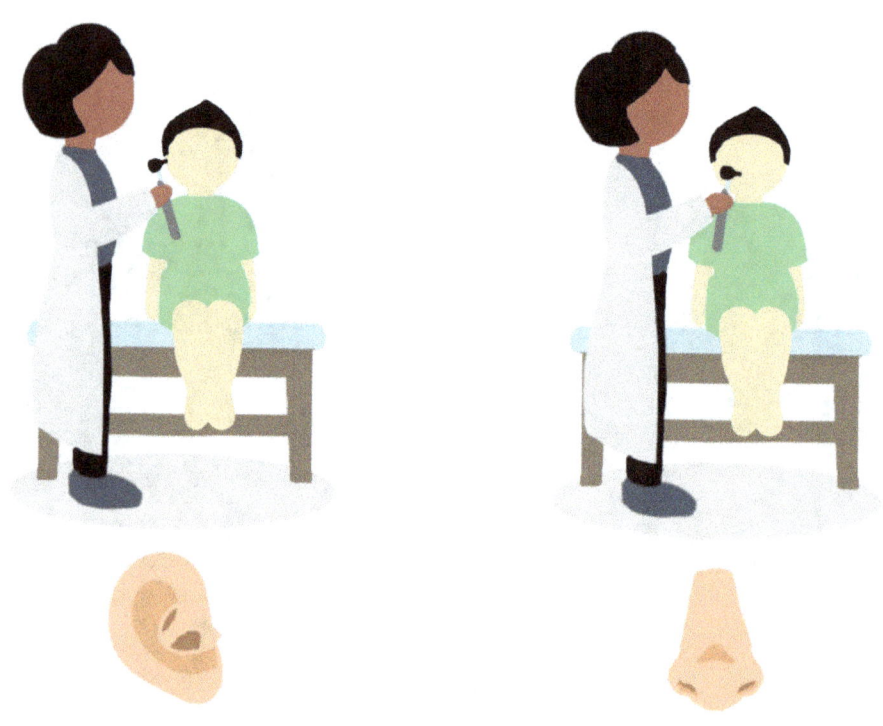

The doctor will look into your ears
and nose with a special tool.

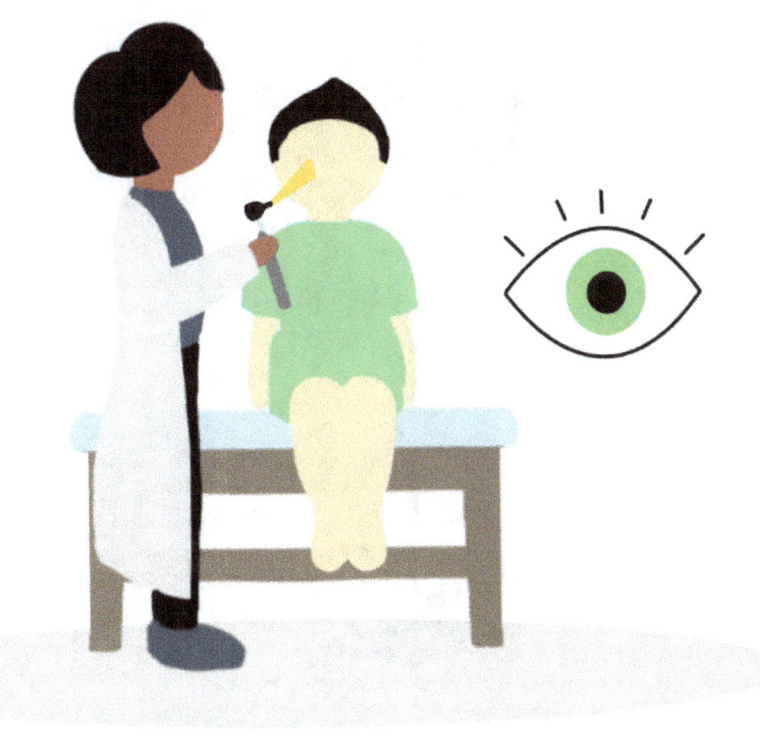

The doctor will look into each of your
eyes with a small flashlight.

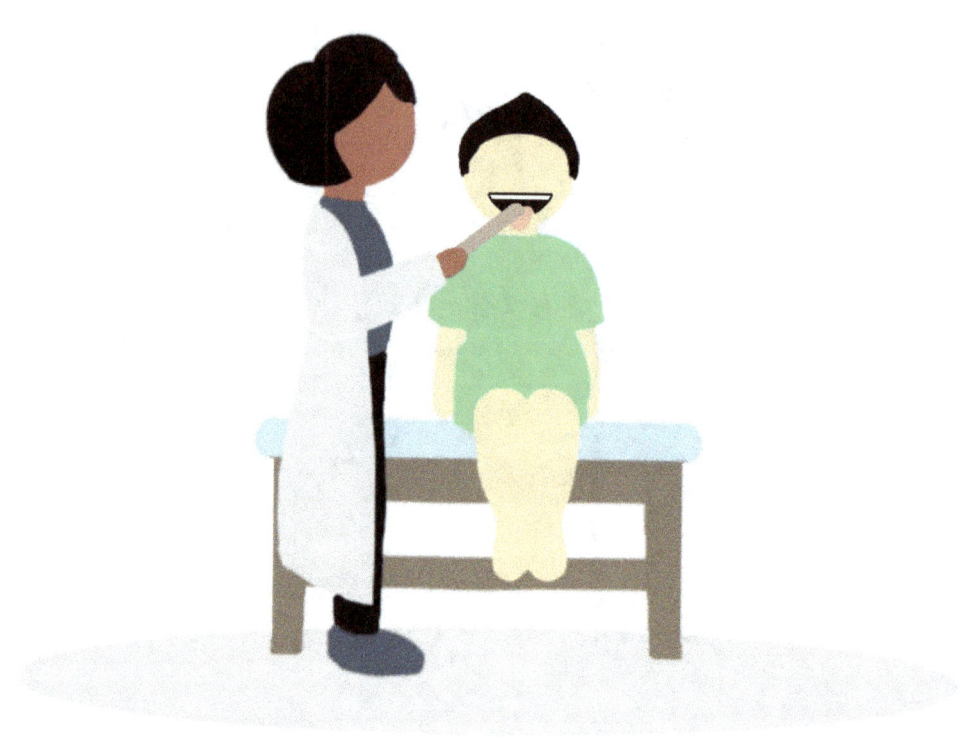

The doctor will look into your mouth. You can stick out your tongue so the doctor can see your teeth and inside your mouth.

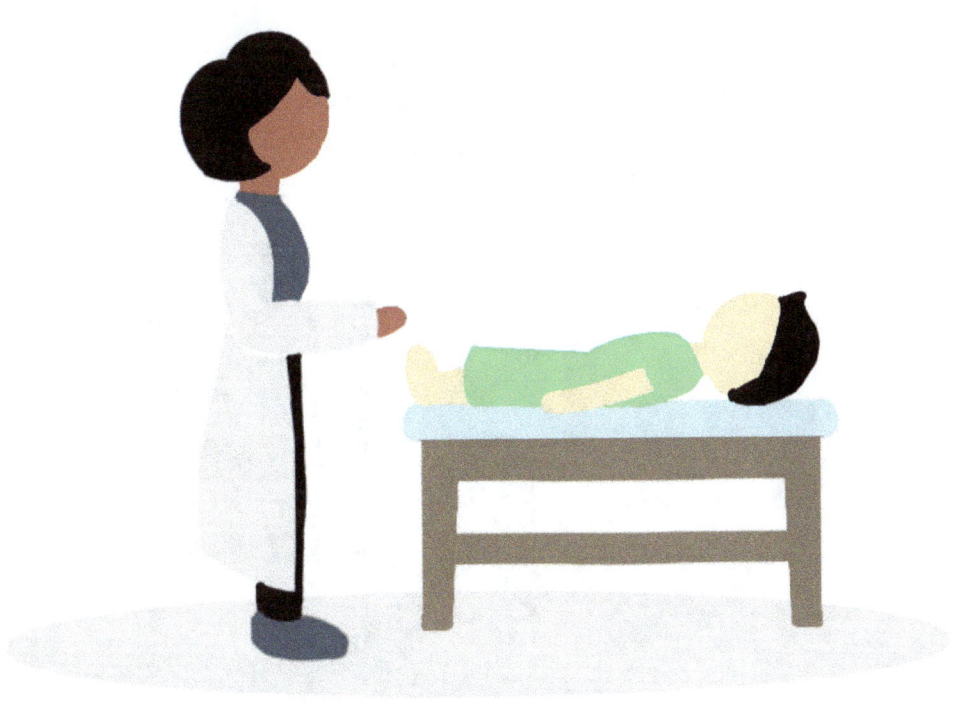

Next, the doctor may ask you to
lay down on the exam table.

The doctor will feel your neck.

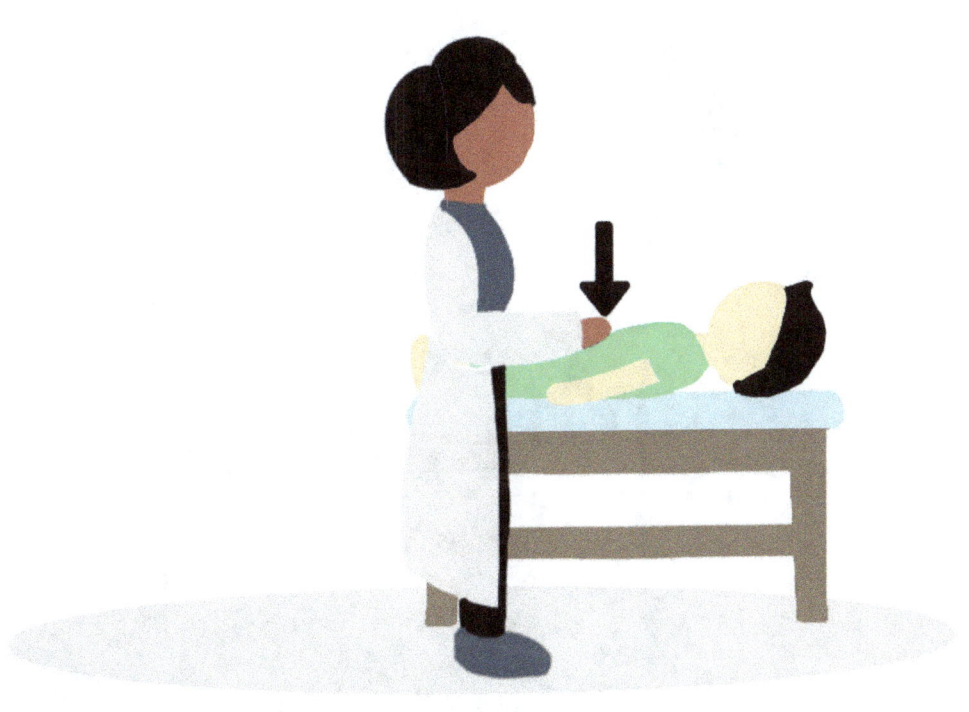

The doctor will feel your belly.

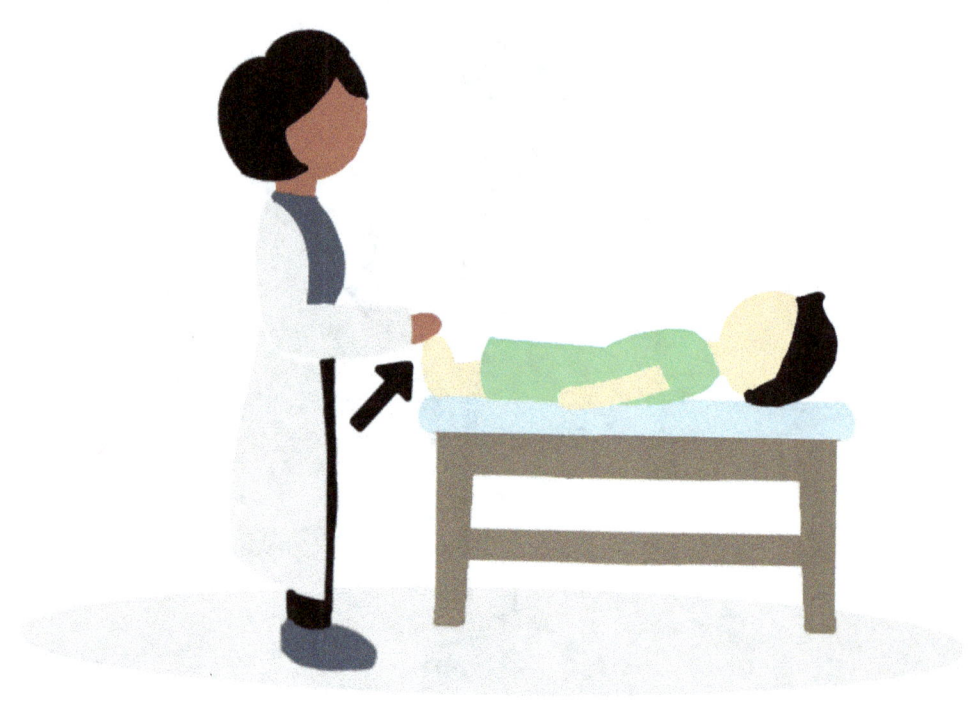

The doctor will feel the skin on your legs and feet.

When the doctor says, "I am all done,"
then you can put your clothes back on.

ALL DONE.
Great
Job!

You did a great job.
It is time to leave the doctor and go home.

Checklist

☐ 1. Arrive at doctor's office.

☐ 2. Go inside and wait our turn.

☐ 3. Nurse calls for us.

☐ 4. Take vital signs.

☐ 5. Go into room.

☐ 6. Doctor comes in.

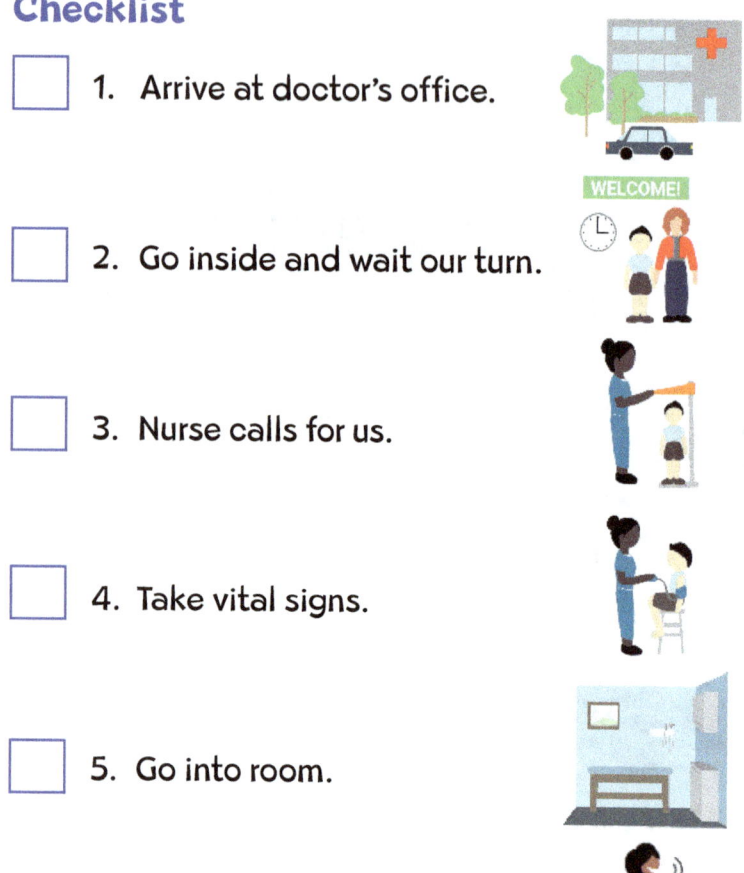

7. Doctor listens to heart and lungs.

8. Doctor looks at nose, ears, eyes.

9. Doctor touches skin.

10. Time to get dressed.

11. All done. Great job

Tape a photo of your reward here.

12. Go home.

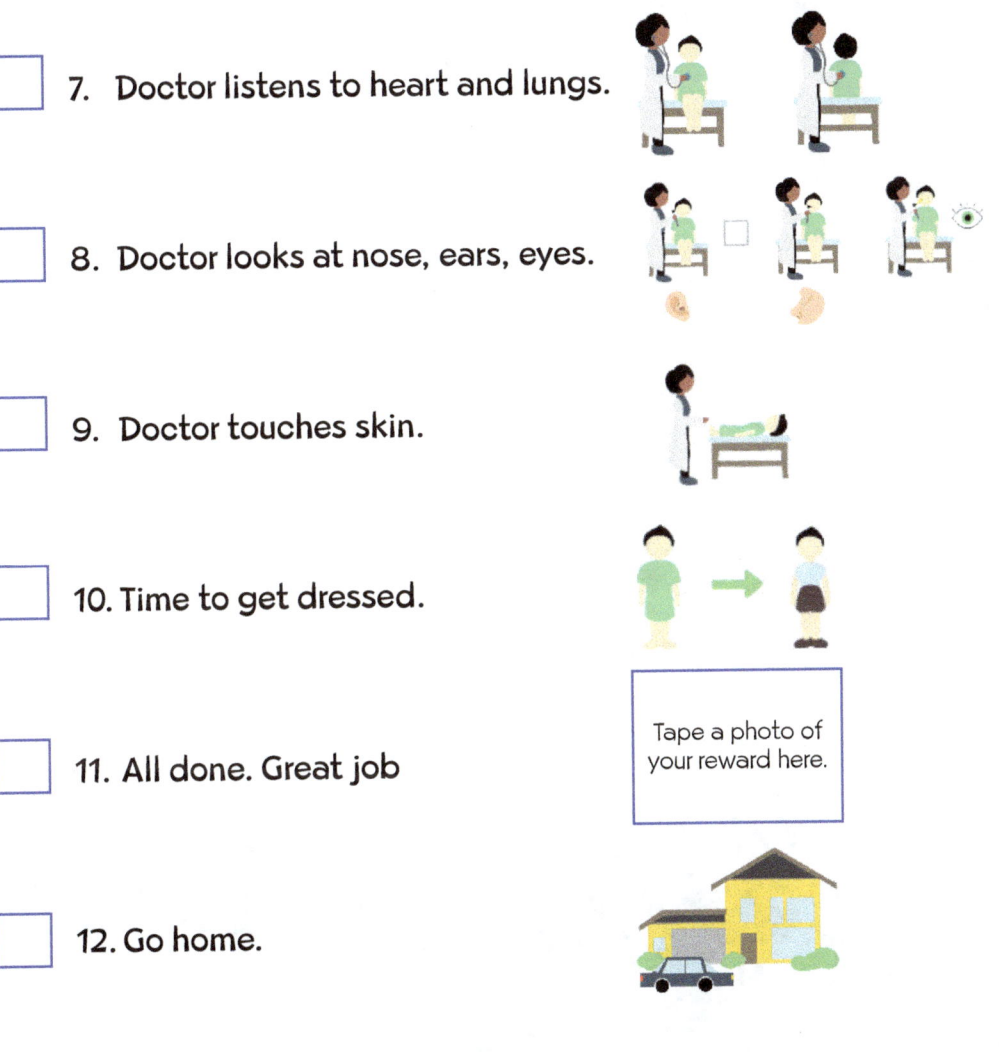

ABOUT THE AUTHOR
Kristine Kenny

Kris has been a pediatric registered nurse for over 30 years, and is presently an assistant nursing professor. Working as a registered nurse in a major pediatric hospital and being the mother of a special needs child, she noticed a huge gap in communication for children with special needs in healthcare settings. She has educated registered nurses at Children's Hospital of UPMC about the proper way to communicate with children with autism in a healthcare setting. She has written multiple stories for her daughter with autism to help guide her through medical experiences for many years. Her passion for education and empowerment is strong. Kris is committed to bringing quality health education for those with unique learning needs. This is the first of many books that will be available.

- Certified Pediatric Nurse and Certified Autism Specialist
- Presentations at Children Hospital of Pittsburgh-UPMC, National Conference- The Importance of Using Communication Tools for Children on the Autism Spectrum in a Healthcare Setting.
- Created an exercise class in her community for teenagers and young adults with special needs.
- Fundraised for Autism Speaks, TRY Special Needs, and TRAILS at Slippery Rock, PA.
- Nursing educator and faculty for 7+ years in RN program, specializing in Pediatric Nurse Care Education and Mental Health Nurse Care Education.
- Practicing RN for 27+ years, specializing in pediatric nursing.